The Perfect Purr

Order this book online at www.trafford.com/06-2183
or email orders@trafford.com

Most Trafford titles are also available at major online book retailers.

Note for Librarians: A cataloguing record for this book is available from Library and Archives Canada at www.collectionscanada.ca/amicus/index-e.html

ISBN: 978-1-4251-0426-9

We at Trafford believe that it is the responsibility of us all, as both individuals and corporations, to make choices that are environmentally and socially sound. You, in turn, are supporting this responsible conduct each time you purchase a Trafford book, or make use of our publishing services. To find out how you are helping, please visit www.trafford.com/responsiblepublishing.html

Our mission is to efficiently provide the world's finest, most comprehensive book publishing service, enabling every author to experience success. To find out how to publish your book, your way, and have it available worldwide, visit us online at www.trafford.com/10510

www.trafford.com

North America & international
toll-free: 1 888 232 4444 (USA & Canada)
phone: 250 383 6864 ♦ fax: 250 383 6804 ♦ email: info@trafford.com

The United Kingdom & Europe
phone: +44 (0)1865 722 113 ♦ local rate: 0845 230 9601
facsimile: +44 (0)1865 722 868 ♦ email: info.uk@trafford.com

10 9 8 7 6 5

The Perfect Purr

102 Cat Poems

Hugh O'Connell

Title cover and illustrations by Richard O'Connell

In memory of three tortoiseshell cats

Peter, Tossel and Scamp

Contents

Cat Sonnet

Such an independent mind
To bemuse, bewitch, bewilder, spellbind:
Winsome and Wary, Nimble and Naughty,
Curious and Charming, Sporty and Haughty.
Surpasses superior smiles,
Assesses us with wise, beguiling eyes.
Always faithful to feline law,
Whether providing peaceful purr or cruel claw.
Every cat a charismatic character,
From frolicking kitten to stalking spectre.
Cat behaviour, at times, so divine:
Onto our laps and into our hearts will climb.
Cats enhance everywhere
And tolerate us as we are.

Cute Kittens

Though enchantingly small,
Don't underestimate them at all.
They can navigate and chart,
Using those sky blue eyes
To override your heart.

Once in your hands
You'll soon understand,
They assume command !
Its curtains for you. Kittens so cute
Make their owners fit like a suit !

Kittens press every single button.
Harness the hardest heart.
Right from the rising of the sun -
So curious, every single one,
And razor keen for all kinds of fun !

Brittle balls of fluff,
Who know how to strut their stuff -
Touching, sniffing,
Looking, hearing, licking.
The world, their toy balloon.

Designed for built-in success.
Like any baby, little puss
Rouses tenderness and defensiveness.
New Mew Few
Hews anew me and you !

A Dog is a Cat's Best Friend !

Into the lounge the owner crept,
Where Bruno the Dog noisily slept.
Next to him she placed a kitten
And left to listen to what would happen.

She waited for Bruno's bark or snarl,
But nothing untoward occurred at all !
When she opened the door she saw
Bruno the dog licking the kitten's face,
As if gravy on a plate !

From that day nothing could separate
What was decreed by Fate -
Cat and Dog passed the test,
And believed each other the very best !

At times, it was quite beyond belief,
When Bruno carried kitty in his teeth !
And when kitty grew older,
Bruno let her ride on his shoulder !

They'd run and play together,
Whatever the hour or the weather !
Their friendship was so deep,
Together they'd eat and sleep.

So, just remember that -
There once was a dog who loved a cat !
And for feline fanatics, even worser,
As it also applied vice-versa !

Casper

Its not a fable but a hard fact.
You need to be aware
Of Casper the Cat,
A beautiful, British blue short hair.

He plays all sort of tricks,
Followed by the warmest of licks.
And so enhances his chances
Of receiving forgiving glances !

A pleasure seeking, loving man,
Who lays on the bed in front of the fan,
Relishing the gust of cool air,
That makes him wriggle, wiggle and purr !

Casper's really one of the boys,
Who carries and drops his toys
Like a winsome wag,
Into the owner's daughter's handbag !

He'd strongly deny he ever begs,
As he rubs himself against ladies' legs
And mews an ever rising song,
Whenever eating time comes along !

He's adept at pulling the bed drawer out,
When he desires to rummage about
Among Very Private Attire,
The owner uses when she wants to retire !

But he doesn't care,
For Casper, Casper is her
Dearest, dearest darling,
Beautiful British blue short hair !

The Perfect Purr

With due respect we wish to demur
From picking a preferred Perfect Purr,
For every cat
Performs that -
As all their adoring owners will concur !

The Moggies of Malyons Road

What makes Malyons Road so unique
Is not its Victorian status, so to speak,
Nor the friendliness displayed by residents
Or the diversity of their accents,
But the quadruped inhabitants who stride
Along this worthy road with such pride,
Supplying a cat cavalcade of unwitting fun
In Ladywell, Lewisham, London !

The Feline Empire is Everywhere - in gardens galore,
Among railings - without impalings !
Behind hedges, before doors, on window ledges,
Wherever a wall, a cat seems installed !
Pavements take second place like a fall from grace.
Cats prefer higher to sleep and retire.
Though all hail from some discreet, demure abode,
Situated along Malyons Road.

Yet no one has reason to complain
About any feline - all bona fide residents, in the main.
Beloved in houses, flats, attics
Which gives blue chipped credibility to their antics !
Yet, also saunter around with such airs,
As if they're Malyons Road true and rightful heirs.
We don't know what they're called,
So we created a game - "New Names For All !"

We've used our eyes to discern personalities
Who've become local cat celebrities:
There's Scary Face, George, Steve, Boss Eyed,
Joe, Pepper, Tigger, Cyril and Maud.
Most are so friendly and say 'hello' with a miaow,
And a few try to follow us wherever we go !
Though we have yet to see a Persian or Siamese,
But think we've half glimpsed a Burmese !

Maude and Cyril live together, and she's renown
For snoring with her mouth wide open !
Steve's claim to fame is that he's really a Big Girl -
Allegedly, the only female ginger tabby in the world !
Boss Eyed would never want to argue or fight,
But still walks straight despite his sight.
Joe is a Big Fat Boy who should be on the telly,
And adores being tickled under his belly !

One or two are more extreme, usually at night,
And capable of giving a Great Big Fright !
Scary Face has a black moustache on a white face,
And behind the hedge near her place,
She gave such a piercing scream one dark night,
The couple passing sped from sight !
Declaring that accursed cat should be certified 'X'
And signed up for Scary Movie 6 !

We must not forget George, who tries so hard
To find a home in Malyons Road.
When folk fetch the milk or the morning post,
George appears, lonely and lost.
Though he's playing a crafty game, of course,
For he tries it on at every house.
But, in the evening, he's no where to be found -
As he's back with his owner and gone to ground !

Last, but not least, consider Pepper and Tigger,
Who live most amicably together.
Pepper is the friendliest cat in the whole universe,
Though Tiger can be a bit perverse !
If he doesn't get attention, he'll skilfully mock-attack
By butting you until you gently interact !
But why not visit Malyons Road, now you know
Its Feline Favourites on Daily Show ?

Cat in the Window

No matter when I roam,
She waits for me to come back home.

She's the star of the show,
Watching for me from the window.

A ball of soft fur
With a swift and quiet purr.

To my humble place,
She bestows beauty and grace.

From her favourite chair
She watches me with a narrow stare.

Night or day,
She never wanders far away.

And when I rest my head,
She also settles down on my bed.

Then wakes me up with a lick
To feed her breakfast - double quick !

She's always near at my side,
Makes me feel I'm part of her pride.

And fills me with a glow
When I return,
Waiting for me in the window.

The Black Cats of Freya

From the Groves of Paradise above,
Where Freya is the Norse Goddess of Love,

She chose an animal to supply
Her chariot to be drawn across the sky !

For a moment, Freya mused and sat,
Before selecting a black coloured cat -

And not one, but two cats for her crew,
To glisten and glow wherever her chariot flew !

The lucky black cats act as a conveyor
To deliver Love Matches arranged by Freya !

Her chariot gleams like a shooting star
Bringing fortune and favour to lovers afar !

So, if you are in love, then you might see
Beyond the roof and beyond the tree -

Freya's chariot blazing across the night sky,
And her two black cats in full mew and cry -

Bringing Freya's blessings from above,
Upon all those who have fallen in love !

Cashpoint Cat

Whenever Wallis makes an appearance
The meanest heart melts at once !
His long haired, smokey grey coat
Every visitor seems to note,
As he wanders outside with the intent
To be the four legged star of the pavement !

Next to the Cotswold Sheepskin shop,
In the flat above the Black Horse Cashpoint,
Wallis descends and chooses to stop
Besides an ever growing queue,
Who never fail to offer Wallis
What he considers his due -

Cashpoint customers seem to understand
That a kindly stroke from their hands
Will hoist Wallis's tail, so he swaggers around
Emitting a rich and resonant purring sound,
That wins a smile from customers of the bank,
Even when their savings have sank !

Smudge Spurns Strangers

Smudge spurns strangers to his house,
And mews to go outside !
Then, defiantly, walks across the road
To display his injured pride.

He sits on the neighbour's drive
Where he makes his attack,
In full view of his home front room,
By simply turning his back !

No matter what time of day,
Smudge continues with his display,
And, there, stubbornly will stay
Until the strangers go away !

The fact she may need friends
Cuts no ice with him,
Nor her relatives or work colleagues.
Smudge loathes all of them !

Its plain to see
He applies his envy like a wedge,
And for any opposition,
Smudge bears an instant grudge.

Until he glares at the departing car
Before skulking home.
Yet starts to purr when he sees
His owner, once more, alone.

King Kong Kat !

With a waist getting bigger
Than his Owner,
You wouldn't want to meet down an alley
The King Kong of Cats -
Mr Thomas O'Malley !

He was brought up as a kitten
In Cardiff City,
And never thinks it a pity
His girth is so great,
He can't set himself up for a date !

But he can open doors
And much more with his huge paws !
After using the garden, he'll rap and tap
The front door knocker
With the belligerence of a boxer !

Mr O'Malley has been described
As 'better than any watchdog alive',
For, if disturbed at night,
The threat of a bite
Would cause any burglar to take flight !

Mr Thomas O'Malley is so big,
The gasman thought he was a dog !
And strangers often err when they see
Mr Thomas O'Malley,
Believing him 'a furry breed of corgi' !

Mr O'Malley doesn't care
Whether folk sigh, snigger or stare
As he so slowly swaggers along -
Due to food so fat,
He's now called King Kong Kat !

There was a Young Cat from Preston

There was a young cat from Preston
Who caught the night train to Euston.

Now, what can we say,
But like any fallen girl in the family way,

Following her 'bit of fun with Tom',
Tibs decided to flee to London.

Love she blamed,
And thought the city would hide her shame.

Though for Tibs there was no escape,
As the guard spotted her at Euston's gate !

Tibs mewed and Tibs cried,
But her request to stay was denied !

For she was Preston's British Rail Cat
And, once labelled, sent directly back !

Sooty

They moved twenty miles away,
    But Sooty traced his way back
To the home where he was raised
    Via path, lane, field, road, track.

He was seen in the back garden -
    A small, black cat peering hard
At the windows where he always sat
    But, now, bizarrely debarred.

When they stepped out, he turned
    And leapt over the garden wall.
Other sightings were sometimes seen,
    Tho' Sooty spurned every call.

His owners put up reward posters,
    But his whereabouts stayed unknown.
They understood and dreaded his loss.
    A cat aghast at strangers in his home.

Brave Bella

As the burglar stealthily climbed the stair
To where Bella's mistress slept in bed,
Bella warily sat on the top stair, acutely aware.

She knew something was badly wrong -
The hooded man was a stranger,
And his behaviour threatened serious danger !

Bella waited before seizing her chance
And then sprang - knocking the burglar
Completely off balance !

The hooded intruder tumbled down
And on the stairway cut his crown,
But managed to stagger back into town !

Bella's mistress woke as if by an alarm bell !
She phoned the police,
Who took blood samples where the intruder fell.

From DNA detected
A violent serial burglar was arrested,
Tried and convicted.

For her demonstration of valour,
The Public Bravery Medal was awarded to Bella,
And her name put
On the City Roll Call of Merit !

Fluff

When we first came here
We saw a smokey grey ball of fluff,
Half-covered by wisteria leaves,
She looked more like a discarded old hat !
Then we were told,
It was Fluff, a little cat, avoiding the cold.

Life for her was tough,
But didn't cower or conquer Fluff.
She weighed hardly anything.
Yet, immediately took to you and me.
She lived permanently outside
At the grand old age of twenty.
Accepted by Tossel, our cat, and slept
On the front door mat, as if our cat !

When tourists strolled past,
They rarely noticed her
Curled up on the gladioli stage,
Below twisting, drooping foliage.
Sometimes she came inside
And slept in a chair before departing
As discreetly as she arrived.

Occasionally, she cheekily stole
From Tossel's bowl. But, one day,
Late in autumn, she disappeared.
When we asked her owner, she shed a tear,
And said she felt Fluff would always be near.
We hoped Fluff had finally found
The highest of high ground.

Mog

Mog was a favourite feline daughter,
Who caused early morning laughter,
When she queued outside
Before taking her turn inside -
To lap the bathroom sink tap water !

The Manor Cat

I'm so glad to have this opportunity
To explain to you my principal duty.
I am aware of my privileged fate
As Resident Cat on the Manor Estate,
I'm also one of the true blue aristocrats,
As I hail from a lineage of exotic cats.

I wear a flowing Blue Persian dress,
To fulfil my duty as the Manor Puss -
The Feline Companion to her Lady,
Who summons me when taking tea,
When I'm asked to sit on my stool
And behave as if I'm also born to rule.

Far from me to ever appear rude
But, some days, I can be in a mood,
Especially at a certain type of guest,
Who never seems to really suspect
That how they behave towards me,
Decides whether they'll return for tea !

Her Ladyship has acquired erratic ways
Which, naturally, differ with the days.
But what remains constant in all of that,
Is the faith she bestows in me, her cat,
Who fulfils her Lady's basic expectation
To quietly listen to her solo conversation.

Other duties occasionally expected -
Catching a mouse suddenly detected.
But I tend to leave such a lowly matter
To traps set by our bloodthirsty butler,
Who I've seduced with subtle guile,
For whenever I see him I purr and smile.

The only complaint I want to make
Is the gardener, who shakes his rake
And declares to his roses I'm a threat,
Or anywhere in the garden I dare to get !
But I maintain its his problem - after all,
I only go there to render nature's call.

My favourite folk are the kitchen staff,
Who love to gossip and have a laugh,
And when I smile and purr so hard
They can't resist carving me a reward -
A cut of beef or tasty tail of fish,
Often placed on a bone china dish !

Other things you might also like to know
Are my midnight strolls, when I softly go
Along the corridors and down the stairs,
Past swords, shields, crests and spears,
In search of kitchen scraps or a cellar rat.
No greater feather could grace my cap !

As you see, its an arduous life for me,
So I often rest beneath the tulip tree,
And listen to the congress of crows
Resident around the east wing windows.
And voices drifting across the lawns,
Near the fountain of nymphs and fawns.

But times move on and I'm not so fast.
Although, when I finally breathe my last,
My Ladyship, surely, will grieve for me
At rest in the Manor Estate Pet Cemetery,
Among His Lordship's dogs and Her Lady's cats -
'Such lovely gals and splendid chaps !'

On Emma,
Returned to An Animal Shelter

They only kept her two days,
Because on hearing song bird displays
Emma mewed to be let out,
And around the garden started to scout.
Until she found
The source of the beautiful sound,
And, then, crept
Up into the apple tree where she leapt
A split second too late,
As the song thrush escaped !
But the owners decided
On birds they preferred to be sided.
So they took Emma back,
Before she launched a fatal, natural attack !

Able Seacat Fred

Of HMS Hecate's crew one came last -
Able Seacat Fred Wunpound,
Mouser, (Second Class),
Who'd never missed a voyage in eight years,
Except on the occasion he disappeared !

The ship had orders to sail and could not fail.
So it left Fred somewhere around the dock,
Then started its Voyage of Really Bad Luck !

Without Fred on board, Doom Loomed !
One engine broke down like an old truck,
Another blew up as if a torpedo had struck !

The potato peeler in the galley
Also went completely do-lalley !

Though they avoided a high sea smash,
When the ship's computer system
And the washing machine both crashed !

After the warship limped into Stornoway,
The captain ordered two of his crew
To scour Portsmouth dock for Fred,
Before the ship's next departure was due !

Fred was found and, as a precaution,
A.B. Wunpound was impounded
In the ship's library before any sailing -
To prevent him going AWOL,
And triggering ill-fortune from Neptune !

So, don't depart without the ship's cat on board,
For its absence you cannot afford !
Tell the skipper, inform the master,
If you want to avoid sailing toward disaster !

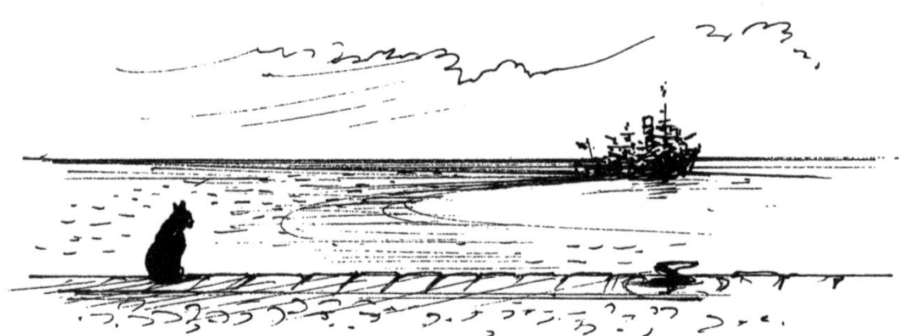

Television Delusion

"They're admiring me !" Pepper's believing,
As she sits upright, smiling and purring.
But half shares the table
With Television Cable,
Which is what they're all really watching !

Tiddles

The Church Cat, 1963-1980

She first appeared in nineteen sixty three
In the churchyard of the village of Fairford.
She emerged from behind the graves
As though she was sent by the Lord !

There, between tomb, cross and stone,
Cried an abandoned, half-starved kitten.
The kindly verger would not let her roam,
And the vicar also agreed to take her in.

They thought and talked and decided
They need a cat for Fairford's great church,
Where the mice were such a problem,
They were using the pews as a perch !

They considered a name for the kitten -
Some were fun, some sounded like riddles.
But the verger decided all the same,
Nothing could quite surpass, 'Tiddles' !

Tiddles proved her worth over the years.
No cat could better seek and search.
Simply excelling at expelling any mice,
Who dared to appear anywhere in church.

Even in services Tiddles was purrfect;
As she often slept on a parishioner's lap,
While hymns and sermons and prayers
Were ideal for helping her have a nap!

For seventeen years Tiddles was known
As along the aisles and pews she roamed.
Thus, the church's feline guardian deserved
To be awarded her own memorial stone.

It was placed not far from the porch,
Where as kitten she was found all alone,
And grew to be as loved as her church,
Where she lies at rest in her sacred home.

Pussini of the Piano !

Led by Aunt Grace, holding a poker,
They advanced along the corridor
To the lounge, where a hideous noise
From the piano filled them with horror !

When they threw open the door
They saw Smuts pressing the keys,
And their fear turned into a cheer !
Though Smuts was not best pleased !

He leapt off the piano and strutted
Out of the lounge with evident disdain.
Although, the attention he received
Soon brought Smuts back in again !

Before long Smuts began playing
As though he was actually entertaining !
His proud owner and friends applauded,
As his velvety paws tinkled or thundered !

Smuts improvised every single score
And loved to conclude with an encore.
Thus, whether playing presto or largo,
He was christened Pussini of the Piano !

Folk smiled and chuckled as they sat,
Listening to a piano being played by a cat.
Some even thought it the start of a new art,
As it was so different to Chopin or Mozart !

To Sue or Not to Sue Mew ?

I think its very nice to sit alone
Quiet and comfortable, safely at home.

Until, Gina, my cat, dozing on the mat,
Suddenly - looks up !

Both ears cocked
And her amber eyes shocked !

What noise has she detected,
Which I never suspected ?

Now I start to strain my ears,
Which arouses my worst fears !

Of the slightest sound I'm now aware -
Was that a squeak on the stair ?

Was that the wind moaning,
Or something in the dark groaning ?

What's that shadow on the wall ?
Shall I give the police a call ?

Monsters and horrors fill my head,
I dread I might soon be dead !

But, when I look down at cat,
She's gone back to sleep on the mat !

Then, I wonder, what about the law ?
Isn't this what its for ?

Here's a first to put to the Legal test -
Aggravated Domestic Stress !

Bringing to book - Disturbing the Peace,
Wilful Deception, Feline False Pretences,

Its historical and hysterical.
Something original, something new.

To sue or not to sue Mew ?
That is the question, I now ask you.

The Old Warrior

An old, scarred Tom
Who slowly ambles along.
He's fought every rival cat in Folly Field,
Until they had to yield,
For Sam relished a fight,
Whether at high noon or midnight.

He never moaned or griped,
Showed the courage of his ginger tiger stripes.
Sam took them all on,
And has the scars to prove he won.
Though at such a cost,
And, finally, old age ensured he lost !

Sam could once erupt,
And wake most of the neighbourhood up !
He'd let out a cry
As though someone had died !
Sam wanted the opposition to know
Into his territory they'd better not go !

At the height of his prime
Sam certainly had a great time:
And seemed without end
To the numbers of eligible girl friends,
With whom he conspired
For new generations to be regularly sired.

Sam's made his name,
And, now, his countless kittens make their claim.
He's no more bold,
For the simple fact Sam is so old.
No longer dominates the scene,
Now pushing the grand old age of sixteen.

He prefers to lay on the grass
And remember victories from long past.
Sam likes to be alone
And somewhere away from his home;
For his house is full of noise
With music and shouting from teenage boys !

Sam strolls around the estate,
Stoically accepting his fate.
His moment over in the sun
With the decline and fall of his kingdom.
Younger toms know he's no threat,
But give him a glance tinged with respect.

He sleeps most of the day
And no longer wants to play.
Though his hunting skills are not all gone
And, before very long,
Quietly, unobtrusively, like a dethroned lion,
Scouts for a quiet home again.

His battle worn face exudes a weary grace
As he seeks a new resting place.
His strong personality
Attracts a certain fan-base popularity.
Older folk sympathise,
He reminds them of struggles in their lives.

Sam finds open a kitchen door
And swaggers across the floor.
The elderly widow does not mind,
She says Sam is 'lovely company to find'.
She knows he's had a 'hard life',
And earned some peace from domestic strife !

So she lets him be,
Until Sam chooses to go home for tea.
But, later, when the sun is low,
Sam returns to the widow's patio,
Where he falls asleep dreaming of places to go,
Only old warriors seem to know.

Pussy Cat Cottage, Mouse Trap Lane.

The resident cat swaggers over her stage:
A stone built, terraced, Cotswold cottage.
She thinks life awfully nice
Especially when chasing mice !

She has a menu of her own.
Her preference for sardines well known.
Though, for a change, will request
Liver and vegetable pellets for breakfast !

Pussy Cat's beds are everywhere -
In all the rooms and even under the stairs !
But in the front bedroom she's usually found,
Sleeping safe and sound.

After a well-deserved rest,
She'll go into the garden to flirt with guests.
Where a couple of toms,
Woo her with off key songs.

Although, if Pussy Cat's not there,
She may be in the bathroom licking her fur,
Or toward a sparrow starting to creep,
Or in some secret place has fallen asleep.

Local mice, of course, complain
About the Pussy Cat resident up the lane,
And in their prayers beg
The owners trade her in for a dog !

Cat Burglar

Holly's head is jet black
With white patches round her eyes,
Which makes her look rather
Like she's wearing a burglar's balaclava !

A description so right !
When, one day, Holly brought back
A child's solitary sock !

Then gloves, handkerchieves,
More socks, shirts with torn sleeves.
Often with clothes pegs attached
To her ever growing cache !

But what made them stare
Was when Holly brought back
Male underwear !
Then it started going too far,
When Holly fetched home a size 40 bra !
Knickers were the very last straw,
The family could stand it no more !

They phoned the police direct,
To turn in their feline culprit !
The station replied, after careful thinking,
To bring Holly along for 'paw printing' !
So, if your missing knickers or bra,
Check out the Washing Line Cat Burglar !

Anti-IT Cat

Its the only mouse
I hope I have in the house,
But Petal would ignore
If I put it on the floor !

While the computer before me
Rouses her envy.
She takes over command
And presses her paw onto my hand.

Computers are Losers,
When Cat chooses
To Declare the Right
To be a Paw and Whiskers Luddite

She jumps onto the keyboard
To wreck all I've done before its stored !
Her claws slide over the keys,
Turns the screen into a kind of Chinese !

The only solution:
Terminate e-mails to the station,
Dump the Internet,
And try not to get too upset !

Remember, remember
Its easier and cheaper to surrender,
For computers will never combat
Victorious, glorious cat !

The Good Cat Family

On a family ramble
They came through the bramble,
And found me in a cardboard box,
Undetected by badger or fox.
From that cold night of yellow moonlight,
Of the kittens five
I was the only one to survive.
The little girl laughed
As her mother wrapped me in her scarf.
I gave my best tiny, heart felt mew,
Unaware I'd found the best of the few.
No longer alone they carried me home,
And from a woolly jumper made my first bed,
Where I lay my weary head.
They gave me a special name - Annabel,
Which I've come to know so well.
From the first day they helped me to play
And, so, I've never wanted to go away.
I've been treated like a family member,
And so many good things I remember.
They've cuddle me whenever I ask
And in the sun lounge I'm encouraged to bask.
I'm fed little treats of fish and meat,
And permitted to sit on favourite seats.
Everything for me they've done,
Nor could I have had such comfort and fun.
When its time, they take me to the vet
To ensure I'm as good as I can get.
They've never complained when I've slept late.
Now, I wonder, if its all to do with fate.

Though I'm now fifteen,
I sense how very lucky I've been
To find a family so kind,
Who've given me such peace of mind.
And if they'd not found me in that box,
I'd have made a tasty snack for badger or fox
Or slowly starved or froze to death,
Instead of having such love, safety and health.
And that's why I've never caused any strife
To the Good Cat Family
To whom I owe my Good Cat Life.

The Mystery of the Missing Cat

Return home. Expect usual reception:
A small miaow. Tail held high.
Several pirouettes on the carpet.

Instead silence reigns. Vacant sofa.
Her body impression on a pillow.
Surely, Scamp must be close by.

But not beneath apple trees or hedge.
Yet, expect her to suddenly emerge -
Tortoiseshell colours among roses.

Informed by my neighbour she was here
In the morning. Afternoon stretches out.
Peer over back gardens, check side lanes.

Its getting dark. Still no sight of Scamp.
Neighbour calls back. Equally anxious.
Fear an injury or trapped somewhere.

No doubt she'll appear in the morning.
Yet, not woken by that dry, sandpapery lick.
Her bowl of food remains untouched.

Once more, at the hedge row call out.
Finally rising in tone to a mighty shout !
But, still, my little cat is not about.

Extend the search even further.
Discover a garden with six chickens
And their owner, a friendly old woman.

Another lonely night sadly face.
Is she trapped in a cold, dark place ?
Did dog or fox win her last, fatal chase ?

Is she feeding from a bin ?
A deeper, darker anxiety settles in -
Convinced she'll never be seen again.

Then, she strolls in through the door
Looking better, fitter and thinner !
Answers every question with a purr.

And, yet, what if a beloved cat pet
Goes missing and is never found ?
No worse thought can a cat lover get.

Our Scamp

When we came home from a night out
Scamp just quietly sat.
A definite change from our usual meeting
With her normal greeting -
Tail in the air, head raised, a cry as if to say,
'Welcome back - please stay !"

But, this time, when Scamp stepped forward,
We could not understand
Why she dragged her hind leg like lead
And her spine was acutely arched.
She sat on the sofa not moving her head.
And looking so scared.

The following morning
Became a source for sudden mourning -
Scamp had a spinal tumour,
Combined with liver failure and a heart tremor.
They put her on a drip,
But we knew from this life she'd soon slip.

Just a little, slim, tortoiseshell cat,
Rescued from a lonely fate.
Until she suddenly fell at thirteen years,
Which wrought tears
At her sudden loss for she so enriched our lives.
Though her memory survives.

Regina v. Felix

When cats wage a Territorial War
There's no use calling in the Law,
For it can only fail
Sending a cat to jail
As it hides five saws in every paw !

Cat Flight World Record Holder

My name is Felix
And I get up to all kinds of tricks !

I break World Records, as you'll see,
For Long Haul Flight journeys !

And, now, it can be told -
Seven times I've flown around the world
Trapped in a Pan Am Jet hold !

Don't ask why
Or how I got trapped -
But 180,00 miles I had to fly !

In 29 countries I landed,
And over a month in each one
I stayed hidden and grounded !

How did I survive to help stay alive ?
By not getting cold
And licking condensation in the hold.

Though I saw so many countries,
None of them impressed me -
For in the hold there's nothing to see !

The USA simply did not please.
I also left some fleas in Los Angeles,
And found no fun in Washington.
Never talked or walked in New York.
San Francisco was no go,
Nor did I see one palm tree in Miami.

I've also been
But not seen the Caribbean,
And Nassau left me hot and sore.

Mexico might as well be a sombrero.
South America made me hysterica -
Rio I no seeo,
San Paulo also,
Buenos Aires I was not awarez,
I quickly quit Quito,
And stayed in cargo in Santiago.

Nor did I cope any better in Europe -
I was sad and hurt
Without a hot dog in Frankfurt,
In Gay Paree I had a wee,
The Swiss I completely missed !
Nor did I roam in Rome,
Russia might as well be in Asia,
And India in Africa,
Of Bombay I have nothing to say,
And in Saudi Arabia, I must assert,
Never once was I offered one dessert !

But London Heathrow, I know,
For there I was discovered at last,
And processed so fast
To a Champagne Flight Home First Class !

The fresh meat was a treat to eat !
And, after I ate, I slept on the jet
With a smile showing how pleased
I was to be going home to Los Angeles !

Where my owner gave me a kiss
In front of the world's waiting press !

Yet, the Exclusive Tale
Of my World Flight Record in the Hold,
To a cat food or fish trade paper
I should have astutely sold !

Not Quite Alone

Nothing moves in the rooms.
Nothing ticks, nor chimes, nor rings.
Not even a drip from a tap.

Static as stone. Silent as a spider.
Still as a funeral parlour.
Over four hours its been like this.

Until, onto the bedroom floor,
a muffled thud. Then, something,
softly descends the stairs.

In the kitchen the occasional tinkle
of pellets in a steel dish.
Though tiny in volume,

they ring like gunshots in the lounge.
A sleek shadow
silently pads across the carpet.

Leaps on the window sill.
No one hears the licking of fur.
There she intends to remain

until the owner occupier returns
to be engulfed
by a purr-filled greeting.

A cat turns a house into a home.

Squeak the Sneak Thief !

Everyone came under suspicion
When the Landlady made her decision -
For she was set on catching
Whoever was snatching
Her bags of pork scratchings !

The landlady declared, even if a local,
Her decision was final !
Whoever the man,
She'd see him in court
And he'd receive a Lifetime Ban !

Bar staff were told to keep an eye
On the display board, and try
To see if they could spot
The cunning culprit in the act.
But no one suspected Squeak the Cat !

Then a cleaner found empty packets
In favourite places used by Squeak,
Who waited till the landlady left,
Then into the bar crept
To commit Grand Pork Scratchings Theft !

On hinds legs he stood, and with his teeth
Pulled off the board three bags per day !
Squeak was labelled, 'A Sneak Thief' !
But from pork scratchings debarred
After they were kept in a screw top jar !

Colour Scheme

in the
back garden
of Twin Cottage

on the dry stone wall,
a tortoiseshell cat
reigns:

half-hidden
by white,
apricot,

pink,
yellow
and scarlet roses.

The Rainbow Cat

Surely, surely you know,
The cat striped like a rainbow ?
Though he's only seen
By those who love to dream.

Its hard to explain,
But this cat looks forward to rain !
He sits on the garden wall,
Awaiting the sign the sky will scrawl.

And his golden eyes glow,
When he sees the rainbow on show.
Then leaps, higher than a lark,
Onto the rainbow when it reveals its arc !

There he'll ride
On the rainbow's striped slide,
And begins to purr
When all its colours cover his fur !

Red, green, blue,
Orange, pink, yellow and purple !
His coat cannot compare
With any other cat anywhere !

He'll pounce and play
On the rainbow till it fades away,
When his coat also loses
The colours the rainbow chooses.

Unable to remain,
He jumps down onto the wall again
To wait, once more,
For the sky to pour and pour and pour !

Accessory Kit Kitty

Miss Bonnie Lavelle Harker
Was not a great looker, heiress or talker,
But she knew to win attention
Needed direct, up-front action !
So she planned to get an Accessory Kit cat
That would vanquish One and All
At the Annual Fashion Ball !
The kitten she chose
Was a burmese blue,
Which she put in her handbag,
Where it whimpered next to her key tag.
Miss Bonnie Lavelle Harker thought by far
He was the best looking guy for miles,
And, so, named him Star.
She knew he'd be a hit
For no-one else would bring
An Accessory Kitty Kit,
Who'd be the Centre of Everything !
So, dressed in her sparkling best,
She greeted her friend, Boris, the host,
Who warily asked,
"Darling, what's that dripping from your bag ?'
Miss Bonnie Lavelle Harker
Thought she'd die as she let out the cry,
"Blast ! It would happen to me !
My Accessory Kit Kitty is having a pee !"
Suddenly, the hostess fell causing a fracture,
After slipping on Star's discharge of nature !

Miss Bonnie Lavelle Harker swiftly departed,
Feeling humiliated and broken hearted.
She, tearfully, drove home alone
And switched off her mobile phone.
But, as she lay weeping on her bed,
Fearing she'd blown her modelling career,
Star appeared and softly licked her forehead.
She gazed at the tiny burmese
And, strangely, started to feel rather pleased.
It was, then, Miss Bonnie Lavelle Harker swore
Star would be her house cat for ever more,
As toilets and Accessory Kit's didn't quite fit,
Causing too many Downfalls
At Annual Fashion Balls !

Bear Facts

Who would have thought a great, black bear
A New Jersey tabby could possibly scare ?
But Jack the cat,
Chased it like a rat,
High into a pine where it growled and glared !

Old Romeo

Tough as oak but smells like an old sock.
Yet still gives a bite like an electric shock !

A scarred nose and half a left ear,
And tends to snarl if you go too near.

But when a she-cat appears,
George hobbles along and brazenly leers.

He remembers when a young lion of old,
His own harem he could win and hold !

Though only George seems to know,
He's still at heart a young Romeo !

Once committed, he starts on cue,
And breaks into a croaky old mew !

She-cats tease him along,
And George thinks he can do no wrong !

But when he gets too close the girls all yell,
For his matted, old coat has a terrible smell !

Although, George still beams,
For he has new girls to court in his dreams !

Brilliant Barney

He's a ginger and white cat,
    Who'd like to be an acrobat !
He has no fear and loves a risk,
    Leaping from table onto desk !

On hind legs Barney stands,
    As though he understands
If you want to stroke his crown,
    No one needs to bend down !

Barney's even got a fit-on seat
    To use the downstairs toilet !
He opens the door on his own
    By leaping up and pressing
                the handle down !

He chases golf balls for fun,
    Yet has still to score a hole in one !
He pulls down the latch to go
    Outside via the kitchen window !

When the car returns he'll sit
    On the warm-as-toast bonnet.
Using his paws he'll hold a fork,
    When the family dine after work !

Yet, even when thought asleep
    And round him people creep,
Barney hears them loud and clear.
    Can you see him turning his ear ?

Ode to Cats

Even asleep on chairs, beds and mats,
    What else quite compares with cats ?
Such feelings they so magically stir
    With a raised tail, tender brush or purr !

Lovely lady, tigerish tom or cheeky chap,
    Fall fast asleep on pillow, table and lap !
No better pet able to encourage a home,
    Within a family or for those living alone -

Who are suddenly and absolutely smitten
    By King or Queen or curious, playful kitten.
Yet, only cats convey an independent air -
    At times aloof, curious, shy, debonair !

They retain their resilient, inherited pride
    And endure where few others could reside.
Their wonders and glories told in true stories
    And still survive after using their nine lives !

Revered by Ancients and Pharaohs of the Nile;
    Persecuted with witches and put on trial;
Decorated for serving in warfare at sea.
    Yet, also needs to be rescued from a tree !

White House and Downing Street residents,
    Praised by Prime Ministers and Presidents;
Raised soldiers and sailors fading hopes;
    Purring under snow white capes of Popes.

Light as ghostly footfalls; scalers of walls;
When in a dash - fast as a lightning flash !
But also keepers of merciless, jungle laws,
When they choose to extend their claws !

Their owners everywhere concur
Every cat has its own unique character.
But cats are not and never ever will be,
Like anything else you'll hear, feel or see !

They softly tread between dimensions,
Able to assume contrasting expressions:
Slumbering royals sunbathing in sunlight
Or raging lions caterwauling at midnight.

What more consummate actor or actress
From All Night Brawler to Playful Puss !
Effortlessly able to play whatever part -
From Howling Banshee to Purring Heart !

How can cat be more suitably described
Than being like Dr Jekyll and Mr Hyde ?
Apparently, so decent and respectable,
But, at night, demonic and disreputable !

Though we, too, bewail, sulk and fuss,
Exactly like some bad tempered puss !
But also charm with a smile and a kiss,
Which shows we're quite similar to puss !

Yet cats have tact and know how to act.
    They even paint and exhibit Cat Art !
Odds on winner when opting to interact,
    Sensing how the hardest heart will react.

They seem to know our emotions so well
    And instantly weave an irresistible spell -
Rouse romance with instinctive elegance,
    So the purrfect bond has every chance !

They easily exceed every expectation,
    In the honesty of their unbridled affection.
They choose their target and then commit
    With a grace and grandeur befitting cat.

And who can possibly resist mewing cries
    Or fail to be bewitched by amber eyes ?
They display a subtle, ubiquitous style
    Captured in their enigmatic, sphinx-smile

Which, down the Ages, supplies the key
    To their secret spirit - vibrant and free !
So, even asleep on chairs, beds and mats,
    Nothing else quite compares with Cats !

Pippin

I must confess its her I prefer.
She does not sulk or demur -
A little, black puss
Who loves a kiss
And, in return, will quietly purr.

Bombay Black Panther

A Bombay black shimmering like Moroccan leather.
  Victor looks like a miniature black panther.
His prowling, amber eyes add to the overall effect,
  At home resides a possible killer suspect.

When a young cat folk stared, unable to believe
  A Bombay black would consent to wear a lead,
Which he did whenever he was taken shopping.
  Until, when older, to a lead he no longer agreed !

His manipulation skills deftly and timely applied -
  He's trained his owner to rise from her chair
When he taps a door; she must, then, open wide
  For Victor to swagger past with a dismissive air.

His favourite response to behave like a little dog,
  When his owner returns home at night -
Standing on hind legs, Victor places his front paws
  On her thighs and miaows with delight !

Yet, Victor has other traits which are not so nice -
  When cuddled, he can sometimes bite !
If he's not satisfied with the position of her lap,
  He'll nip his owner until she gets her seating right !

Though Victor 's become a beautiful Bombay black,
  He'll scowl and glare with pantherish disdain
At those who resist his wants, whims or wishes,
  As if, in this world, they'll not long here remain !

Very Nervy, Wary Barry

A true, home cat -
Simply terrified of what might
Lurk out there,
Whether its day or night.

Lives on his nerves
And dead easy to scare -
Scurries away,
Even if other cats just stare !

Cherishes our company,
Stays by the fire, rarely goes out.
Yet runs and hides
Should any of us dare shout.

Highly strung
In that very-special-cat-like-way.
Incapable of adjusting
To household appliances night or day:

The vacuum cleaner,
Whisk, drill or washing machine,
Ensures Barry,
For hours, will not be seen !

Don't mention thunder !
Barry cowers under the chair.
Mews and whimpers,
Dangles in a chasm of despair.

Barry's no hero,
But we don't care about that.
We just adore
The gentle nature of our cat.

Vet Visit

A Jack Russell strains towards the door.
Confused that a walking trip should end
In a room crammed full of serious people.

The cat owner appears most ill at-ease.
Whispers to his cat under a towel draped
Over a cage. Her mews upsets a boxer.

The grey haired vet appears. Greets them
With cheery words. Owners offer thin smiles.
The shrouded cat releases a rumbling growl.

On entering the Examination Room, the cat
Snarls. They use the towel to extract the cat
Who hisses, spits and snarls at the Vet.

The owner clutches his cat, whispers to her.
Still she growls. Instinctively senses danger.
Here - nothing and no one will she ever trust.

The Vet scrolls her history on the computer.
Under his hands she finally settles as he
Inspects eyes, teeth, paws, fur, tummy, tail.

Her annual injections hardly take a minute.
The vet declares she's fine. After payment,
Pet and owner depart. Less stressed.

Clarissa and Me

She's my one and only pet
And to her I really owe such a debt.

My family has grown up and gone away,
So we're left alone day after day.

We're both clearly aware
That we each have our favourite chair.

We've shared fears and tears,
And been together for years and years.

She's calm and good and kind,
And none of my views seems to mind.

She never goes out to fight
And keeps me company every night.

She never makes a mess,
Nor any kind of unnecessary fuss.

Yet, when all is said and done,
We've also had our moments of fun -

Rolling balls of wool across the mat
Delights Clarissa, my long hair cat.

Even when the wind is high,
Her purr sounds to me like a lullaby.

And, then, when I close my eyes,
Once more I see a world full of smiles.

Smokey Joe, The Stow Shop Cat

His youth long gone,
But Smokey Joe's the silent partner,
Like the moon to the sun -
A steady, sturdy sort trusted by the owner,
Who always tries to remember
His birthday on the fifth of September !

Like some special guest star
Among brushes, teacloths, canvasses, paints,
Cards, crayons, calendars,
Oil kits, pencils and pens, a gamut of gifts,
Smokey Joe sleeps - blissfully unaware
Of how customers stare !

On daily display:
A black coat with an undercoat of white fur,
Who falls asleep most of the day.
But, when he wishes, will suddenly purr !
Tho' some customers only remember the shop
For Smokey Joe sleeping a lot !

Open at ten and closed at five,
Yet Smokey Joe's the kind of wily cat
Who knows exactly how to survive.
But, besides that,
When Smokey Joe descends into a mood
For several days he'll sulk and brood.

In the evening he'll take a garden stroll,
Tracks a dove flying around,
Who settles on top of the washing pole.
But Smokey Joe's paws stay on the ground,
Close to the house,
Hoping to feast on a late night mouse !

When the moon climbs high Smokey Joe
Knows its time to go.
He ambles back in and gently lays his head
On the woolly blanket of his bed,
And wonders who'll stop
To stroke his head tomorrow in the shop.

Slippers and Mr President

Let us return to nineteen hundred and six,
When President Theodore Roosevelt
Was the incumbent in the Oval Office
And Slippers, his favourite six toed cat.

One notable occasion still stands out -
A State Dinner at the White House.
Tables glistened with bone china and silver,
Without a sign of one single mouse !

Standards exceeded every expectation -
The White House glittered at its very best !
It easily rivalled Europe's royal coronations
And suitably impressed its titled guests!

The Guest List for such an Occasion
Read like the Who's Who of Diplomacy -
Ambassadors and Prime Ministers,
Dukes and Duchesses of the Aristocracy !

Gentlemen arrived wearing top hats and tails,
Ladies dazzled in diamonds and pearls,
Trailing silk gowns like glistening sails,
Escorted by Senators, Generals and Earls.

Following a memorable State Dinner,
The President, with the wife of an ambassador,
Led the Procession to the East Room,
Down a long and wide gleaming corridor.

Ambassadors, ministers and plenipotentiaries
    Chatted happily as they proceeded,
Totally unprepared for what happened next -
    When, suddenly, their way was impeded !

Half way down the corridor, the President
    Espied something familiar in their path.
It was none other than Slippers, his cat,
    Laying fully stretched out on the carpet !

Slippers simply beamed and purred,
    Lapping up whoever he could attract !
It was perfectly clear Slippers wasn't moving,
    As he gladly rolled over onto his back !

The Great and the Good and the Wise
    Had been halted by a bundle of fur !
And never could anyone have ever thought,
    A mere cat exerted so much power !

Mr. President was about to pick up the cat,
    When the cat allergic lady beside him shuddered !
The President knew he had to think quick
    Or the whole occasion was scuppered !

The President bowed to his partner before
    Deftly guiding her around the cat,
Who proclaimed with a purr his approval,
    As the Champion of the Carpet !

After the United States, came Great Britain,
France, Germany, Holland, Spain
And other nations from all over the world,
Who skirted Slippers as if a mountain !

So, if you're ever asked, "What halted
Half the world and Mister President ?
Reply, "Slippers, The White House Corridor,
All Conquering Tom Cat Resident !"

Skyscraper High Diver !

From her New York apartment in the sky
Coco fell from thirty two floors high !

On the side walk they sighed,
When Coco hit they expected her to die !

But things were not about to get messy,
For Coco triggered her arboreal ancestry -

When, in mid-air, a cat's muscles relax
And trigger 'an acutely refined gyroscopic reflex' !

Like a flying squirrel in full splay,
Coco put on an equivalent display -

So the potentially fatal 'splat flat' result
Was averted as Coco descended like a parachute !

Her survival skills affirmed by medical proof,
For she only had minor thoracic injuries
and a chipped tooth !

Forty eight hours later, Coco, once again,
Was surveying like Catwoman New York's skyline !

And the twinkle in her sea blue eyes,
Showed she still banked several of her nine lives !

Urban Singleton

I work all day for my car and flat
And my best friend, Jenny,
My little white cat.

I get home at seven
And when I open the door,
Jenny is waiting with a smile and purr.

From the micro wave
I extract a pre-packed meal for one,
Which I eat while watching television.

Jenny sits beside me
On my calf leather settee,
Quietly keeping me company.

I don't need yoga to unwind,
Its Jenny I find
Who relaxes my body and mind.

I prefer Jenny to a bloke.
And I don't joke.
She doesn't lie, swear, drink or smoke.

She hardly costs any cash
And, unlike with men,
It won't be a relationship car crash.

In fact,
All girls should get a cat.
Sweeter and safer than a two legged rat

Cat Call

Cleo is a truly classic Siamese cat,
Who simply loves to orally interact.
So, when far from home,
To her owner on the phone,
She'll purr and mew, chuckle and chat !

Golf Ball Kleptocatmaniac

Tommy was a black cat from Weston-Super-Mare
Of whom a local golf club was very much aware !
The fifteenth hole was their most difficult shot,
Made worse by Tommy, who tried to stop every putt !

From cover amply afforded by a small laurel bush,
Tommy would calculate when to make a sudden dash !
And before the ball fell into the hole (as it should in golf),
Tommy would grab it and run of with it in his mouth !

A player finally chased the cat back to his house,
Where the owner said Tommy preferred a golf ball
to a mouse !
And, also, admitted that in the previous year, all in all,
Tommy had brought home over five hundred balls !

In fact, they were tired of finding golf balls everywhere:
In pots and chests, under beds, cabinets and chairs.
Nowhere was immune - in the garden or in the home,
From wardrobe to desk, to behind every gnome !

But they couldn't give Tommy the Cat the sack,
As he was a dedicated, golf ball, kleptocatmaniac !
How could they tell Tommy it shouldn't be done,
When he, at least, seemed to be having such fun ?

So, the owner and the club agreed that from there on,
Every golf ball that Tommy brought back home,
The club, in return, would wait to get it back !
But hoped Tommy wouldn't then double his attack !

Jam Jar Cat

We know the following verse
    May cause our readers' distress,
But if you feel any stress,
    How do you think felt this Puss ?

'Pickles' was named after the 'incident',
    And you'll see it was appropriate -
When a jam jar was pushed over
    His head - hoping he'd suffocate !

Though Pickles was a clever cat
    And escaped by smashing the jar
On the pavement, but that left
    Around his neck a jagged glass collar !

They kept him in the rescue home -
    He was the only cat they ever did -
For whenever he spied a stranger
    Pickles rushed into his hutch and hid.

Billy, the Car Cat

Have you heard of Billy ?
    His conversation is such fun.
It doesn't matter who you are,
    He's a friend to everyone !

Billy shows what he feels,
    For he likes to miaow and chat;
And when he smiles he reveals
    He's also a one tooth cat !

He's a cuddly, ginger puss
    Now in his fourteenth year,
Who loves nothing better
    Than a ride in the family car !

He's game to go anywhere
    And to travel slow or fast.
But always starts to purr
    Whenever a lorry is past !

Billy mews with delight
    Like a Roadie Feline Star,
When passing passengers wave
    At the tabby cat in the car !

Whether home or away,
    Billy adores company,
And, I think, given the chance,
    Would love to live in a taxi !

King Cat

Define 'cool':
Think Cat.
No need do more
Than that.

*

Define 'style':
Nominate Cat.
Got more per millimetre
Than any other creature.

*

Define 'charisma':
Again, name Cat.
Who, what, when, where,
Can possibly compare ?

*

Define 'perfection':
Cats excel inspection -
Grace and grandeur,
Motherhood and murder.

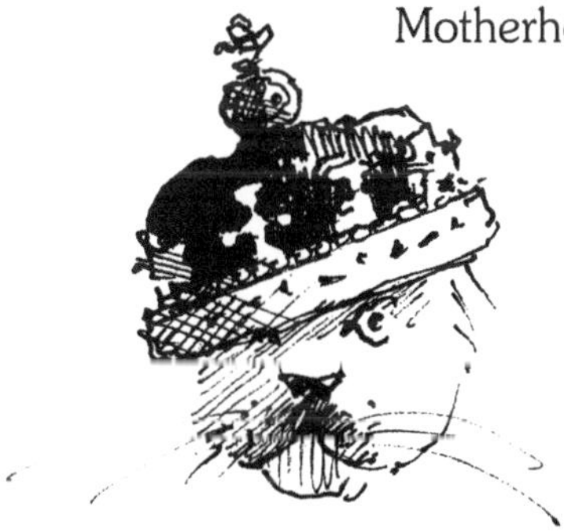

Sonnet to Bastet

Who leapt from the Eye of the Sun
And, yet, is also a furry ball of fun ?

Who stalks the Midnight Moon
And, yet, can be alert at high noon ?

Who is the Symbol of Gold
And, yet, not one gram doth hold ?

Who conveys the Purity of Virginity
And, yet, thrives on nightly lascivity ?

Who ensures the Blessing of Fertility
And, yet, prizes solitary individuality?

Who displays Olympian Agility
And, yet, cultivates absolute docility?

Who was hailed an Egyptian Goddess
And, yet, we can still hold and caress ?

'Bastet' - Egyptian Goddess of the sun, the moon, virginity, good health, fertility; represented by a sitting cat.

Get Off My Lap !

Get off my lap, you dratted cat,
I've things I have to do !
Wash the dishes, sweep the mat,
And clean the loo !
How will I do any of that
With you plonked on my lap ?

Get off my lap, you rotten cat,
I'm a busy person you know !
And hardly time to sit down and chat
When there's so much to do -
Windows to clean, beds to make,
And pillows to shake !

Get off my lap, you lazy cat,
I'm not the type to be messed around !
Why can't you go and catch a rat
Instead of settling down ?
I've a letter to send
And a back garden to tend !

Get off my lap, you useless cat,
You've put me right out of my stride !
If I stay here I'll just get fat
Which will ruin my diet guide.
When I get up,
I'll definitely get a very active pup !

Get off my lap, you wretched cat,
You're getting in my way !
I should put on my coat and hat
For I've planned to do the shopping today !
I've also been thinking,
Why should I buy you any more chicken ?

Get off my lap, you cunning cat,
I know your sly old game !
You don't want me to buy that flat,
So your safe, little life can stay the same !
But I want to get out of this place,
As I feel my life is going to waste !

Get off my lap, you boring cat,
I want to meet new chums !
You're quiet and kind but certainly lack
The ability to converse with old mums !
And don't so sweetly sigh,
As if you adore laying on my thigh.

Get of my lap, you silly cat,
You're stopping me having a life !
What's wrong with the mat ?
Why do you cause me trouble and strife ?
And just because I stroke your fur,
There's no need to persistently purr.

Get off my lap, you sleepy cat,
Can't you see this isn't my idea of fun ?
While I've been sat,
So many jobs I should have done !
But, worse still, now you've fallen asleep,
I find I'm also counting sheep !

Get off my lap, I say yet again !
Though, the heat she generates
Eases my rheumatism.
But she so infuriates,
She's exhausted me laying on my lap.
So, I, too, must take a little nap !

A Dart for a Cat is like a Stick for a Bow Wow

You never could tell
Who'd walk into the Black Swan Hotel
Back in Newcastle upon Tyne in 1939.

A young stray cat strolled in one afternoon,
And when it saw darts being thrown,
Behaved like a dog after a stick, ball or bone !

Would you believe,
All three darts thrown into board
The stray cat immediately began to retrieve ?

The cat was shrewd, too,
Pulling each dart out with her paws,
So they slipped harmlessly onto the floor.

Then, with her teeth, picked up each one
And returned it to the player,
As if it was something she'd always done !

Soon Kitty was in the dart's team
Sitting on the scorer's table, ready and able
To retrieve all darts for a bowl of cream !

So, remember this feline dart team member,
If ever asked, "When and How
Is a Dart for a Cat like a Stick for a Bow-Wow ?"

A Bit More Lilac

Ben, a Lilac Point Siamese kitten,
on spotting the bathroom door ajar,
ran across the floor.

She just managed to hoist herself
onto the toilet pan.
But, then - without further ado -
fell headfirst into the loo !

SPLASH !

Cries forlorn
were heard from deep within the pan !
She felt a terrified fool -
about to drown in the tiniest pool !

But Dad rushed in
and fished out the kitten !
Then warned Ben,
next time he'd pull the chain !

Though Mum had a major concern
that Ben might have swallowed poison,
due to 'lilac blocks' in the cistern !

She phoned the Vet who declared,
Ben would not get sick,
But 'might turn a bit more lilac !'

Princess Soraya of Persia

No point trying to cast any aspersion
Against Soraya whose thoroughly Persian.

Her coat's smokey grey with a tinge of black.
And her blue eyes glare as if about to attack.

Princess Soraya rarely wants to play,
Adores laying around most of the day.

She openly loathes noisy children,
Far prefers quietly-spoken women.

She moves with effortless grace
And in a palace would not be out of place.

She remains perfectly aloof and cool
And detests those who play the fool.

Nor would she deem it dignified
To pursue a mouse in the garden outside.

She expects choice bits in her china dish -
The best cuts of meat and fish.

Her arrogance some judge immense.
What could possible be in her defence ?

Simply this - she's never caused any harm,
Nor can anyone can resist her regal charm.

No matter how great the adversity,
Nothing overshadows her personality.

Princess Soraya fills the house with such style
By applying her swagger and superior smile.

Nightmare Cat

I hear him caterwauling late at night
Which really gives me quite a fright !
I see him so clear,
It fills me with fear
And his silver claws shine so bright !

I also hear him snarling in the day.
His black spectre never goes away.
Where ever I'm found
He'll track me to ground.
Am I forever to be his only prey ?

Its hard to understand or to explain.
His pursuit of me will always remain !
Its sure not nice
For any mice
As we've nothing to possibly gain !

Cat Layabouts

Why do cats layabout
When they really should be out ?
Why does a cat lay its head,
Where there shouldn't be a bed ?

They'll sleep in a cupboard or drawer,
Even behind the settee on the floor !
They've even been seen
Fast asleep inside a washing machine !

They actually think they've a right
To sleep anywhere they like !
As for Bedrooms, what can we say ?
Most would lay there night and day.

Its as though they simply don't care
That its OUR bed, settee and chair !
Something here is radically wrong -
As if OUR possessions to THEM belong !

In fact, cats should show us some respect,
Then, maybe, we might not get so upset !
Though, its true for both men and women,
Cats, invariably, end up owning them.

Although, as long as they cause no harm,
Surely, that's part of their charm ?
I suppose we might as well admit,
Cats have got us beat !

But, there again, I'm sure you'll concur,
Who can be cross for long
With either a Him or a Her,
When they start to mew and purr ?

Cartoon Doom !

Surely, a trillion to one chance,
What happened to a cat in Nevers, France.

A peaceful, happy puss who'd never done
Any harm or hurt to anyone.

Until that afternoon in the front room,
When watching a Tom and Jerry cartoon.

As Tom madly chased Jerry round the place,
The family cat displayed a wicked face -

And also began racing round the room,
Chasing the children, Dad and Mum !

The children yelled while the cat spat,
Keen to launch a fresh attack !

Mum rushed out with the children,
Just before the cat leapt at them !

Dad managed to grab a life-saving chair
To fend off the cat's fiendish claws !

Mum phoned the police who soon came
And witnessed a cat no longer tame !

It hissed and growled, snarled and spat,
But was finally trapped in a net !

No one explained why the cat went mad,
Who had to be put down, which was so sad.

P.S.

A tale to depress Tom, I guess,
But would make Jerry ever so merry !

The Mother

She mews around the room,
Scratches every cupboard door;
Wondering why she's unable to find
Her four kittens anymore.

She barely nibbles her food.
Then, retraces her steps,
Scouting like a lioness for her cubs.
Her searching hardly stops.

She gets more and more distressed,
Listening for the tiniest sound.
Unaware those trying to comfort her,
Drowned her brood in the pond.

Simon

Recipient of the Dickin Medal, 1949

When Communist guns opened fire
On HMS Amethyst,
A shell killed the Captain
And singed the whiskers and fur of Simon,
The ship captain's cat.

Simon was in a state of shock
And for a few days could not do a lot,
But he noticed the shelling cracks
Revealed new hiding places
Of the ship's rats.

Simon was soon back in action
And caught a record number of victims,
Exceeding all expectation !
Opinion from the crew
Declared Simon was a hero !

He kept adding to his Rat Hit List,
As HMS Amethyst
Made its famous escape at night
Down the Yangste River
To the open sea and sunlight !

A hero's welcome in Hong Kong
Was delayed by quarantine,
But Simon so pined for crew and ship,
From life he slowly slipped.

Yet Simon's service was known to all,
And was posthumously awarded
The Dickin Medal -
The animal equivalent of the V.C.
Whereupon Simon leapt, gloriously,
Into Royal Navy history.

The Snob Cat

The kind of cat to cause an owner hysteria,
    That's what we say about our Gloria !
Every room she thinks she enhances,
    And casts us the snootiest of glances !

Despite given pride of place on the sofa,
    Gloria is certainly not won over !
She growls if she's picked up too quick,
    And into your hand her claws can stick !

Her mood is certainly not improved
    Even with the very best kind of food.
Sardines or kippers are no good,
    She wants song birds from the wood !

Gloria expects someone to open the door
    Or she'll scratch it with her claws!
She'll not sit in the same room as children,
    Deeming them more trouble than a kitten.

Her basket had a hand-knitted shawl
    But that did not appeal to Gloria at all -
So she ripped it to shreds and then slept
    In the spare room reserved for guests !

She rarely goes outside, even on the grass,
    For other cats she might have to pass.
All of them she deems no better than outcasts,
    Not even a siamese is in Gloria's class.

She's convinced that she's an Aristocat,
Having next to an Abyssinian once sat.
But she's really only a tabby grey and black,
And her parents wouldn't have her back !

Her la-di-dah airs and snooty graces
Owe more to back alleys than palaces !
But Gloria really should be on the stage,
For she's breathtaking when in a rage !

Its been known for Gloria to briefly enter
And, if she disapproves of a visitor,
She'll turn right around and walk snootily out,
As if there's a bad smell about !

For us she really does not seem to care
With her snout raised right up in the air !
She only likes Mum when it suits -
Like playing with the wool she knits !

Its hard enough as things are -
She sulks when we go out in the car.
And when we return, our family puss,
Simply turns her back on all of us !

Her disdain is, in short - immense,
So what, possibly, is in her defence ?
She can fill the lounge with such style
With a swagger and a supercilious smile.

Although, we think it can only get better
When Gloria has her own bed-sitter.
There she could choose to be good or bad,
With less chance of driving us mad !

Yet, none of us would dare to try to explain
Why Gloria could no longer remain !
In fact, that solution is not very clever,
We'd all be in the doghouse for ever !

We're all quite resigned to her growling,
Whenever she thinks standards are falling,
Casting a frosty, yellow-eyed glare,
Before falling asleep in her favourite chair.

So, Gloria continues in her self-appointed job,
As the greatest and haughtiest cat snob !
And even dreams of a statue like Queen Victoria,
As a fitting tribute to the Reign of Gloria !

Tale of Tails

Their mother rushed across to them
To scold her terribly cruel children -
'Its only a kitten,' she wailed,
'Don't hold it by the tail !'
'We're not ?' they replied. 'Its his stem !"

Sesame

The saddest runt you ever saw:
Born with no eyes and a hingeless jaw.
A most distressing birth, plus a tooth
Jutted out of the side of its mouth.

No future for him could the vet see.
He'd die if stung by a wasp or bee.
The vet judged the runt of little worth,
Advised putting him to sleep at birth.

Yet being both blind and disfigured,
Caused deeper emotions to be triggered:
As one the family agreed on their action -
They gave the runt life long protection.

Their devotion plain to see, even then,
When their son bathed the eyes of the kitten,
Saying, "Open Sesame !" Hence his name,
Which was greeted with such acclaim !

They kept him on a twelve foot lead when
He warily began to smell plants in the garden.
Sesame still purrs when he sniffs grasses
And knows the footsteps of whoever passes.

Around the house he'll happily go walking,
Adores attention and social interacting.
He'll place a comforting paw on mum's hand,
Tho' Dad's chosen to sink into slumberland.

And, so, from the runt of the litter, Sesame
Was welcomed into the heart of the family,
Who saw beyond and above his disabilities,
While he further enriched their finest qualities.

My Cat

I love her best when she purrs
    As I hold her in my arms.
She never snarls or demurs,
    Only enchants with her charms.

I love how she climbs up on me
    To lick and kiss my face.
Her tender affection plain to see -
    A quiet delight about the place.

I love the aroma of her brown fur
    And her four snow white paws.
Her ready play, her pleasing purr
    And gentle kneading of her claws.

I love how she listens to me,
    Devoid of boredom and guile;
And offers elegant company
    With a wise and kindly smile.

Fred's Fantastic Fate

Despite his name, Fred's a 'she",
And there are greater surprises yet to be -
For Fred's owner did not want to delay,
She wanted Fred 'put down straight away' !

Madam was off to the South of France,
But Fred would not be given the same chance.
Until her neighbours from Wolverhampton
Decided to make a day trip to Bourton.

They told of Fred's doom to 'Only Cats',
And Austin declared they must avert that !
Cat lovers are filled with strife,
When they think a puss may lose its life !

So, in their shop window could be read
An advert seeking a home for Poor Fred.
They were on the edge of despair,
Wondering if they could find any one to care !

But, then, 'Only Cats' owners heard
A new home had been found for Fred !
From Wolverhampton she was driven
To a place they hoped would be her haven.

A few weeks later a card arrived
And the 'Only Cats' owners were surprised !
For Fred's new home - you'd never guess -
Was BLENHEIM PALACE, no less !

Fred found a Grand New Life not slaughter,
With the Head Butler and his daughter.
She loves the sofa and her bed
And is simply purrfect playing Aristocat Fred !

Shadow

How could anyone fail to guess
The jet black kitten was homeless ?
A home she had been trying to seek,
Every desperate day of the week.

She mooched around a glowing Inn,
But no-one there would take her in.
Tho' Luke, a young boy, noticed her,
And in his heart compassion stirred.

He walked past the Inn every day
And noticed the kitten did not go away.
She mewed at every passing stranger,
And cars parking were a constant danger !

Luke first checked with the Inn,
Did they own the jet black kitten ?
"No way. No chance," they said.
"Our Alsatian would bite off its head !"

Then, on a cold, wet, windy evening,
When to home Luke was returning,
He saw the kitten mewing alone,
And decided he must take her home.

The six foot tall young man
In his hands cupped the kitten,
Who purred then sucked his finger.
No longer near the Inn need she loiter !

Luke's mother welcomed the tiny cat,
But noticed her claws did not retract.
Was this the reason why
She'd been cast out to die ?

But that would not be done
By this kindly mother and son.
They offered their home to the kitten
Who was, at once, totally smitten !

She followed Luke wherever he'd go,
And so was christened, "Shadow" !
When she nestled under his chin,
A black beard suddenly appeared on him !

Yet, in the beginning, the kitten
Recoiled from contact with women.
They thought that a clue, at first,
About a possible problem in the past.

But Shadow soon lost her unusual fear,
And tracked Mum like a shadow so near.
Though she loved to lay on Luke's bed,
And sleep right next to his head.

The little, jet black cat's main mystery
After nine years was - she stayed so tiny.
She'd hardly grown since the day
Luke brought her back from harm's way.

What other feline physique could cap
An adult cat in a kitten's body trapped ?
Yet, never displayed any fear or pain,
And with her rescuers gladly remains.

Her restriction in size well known,
Though her heart has certainly grown -
From the love she's been shown
By a loving family in a loving home.

Mice Mansion Takeaway

Now, you guys must come round
To the pad I just found
Which is a mound that'll astound !

An old mansion
That's seen some action !
But, now's in a state of dereliction !

Straight away I could tell
Things have not gone well ,
For its cold, dark and has a musty smell !

Its sure not nice,
Over run with fleas and lice,
But also has an Empire of Mice !

Its true what l say - mice supply me
With six hot meals every day !
So why not visit Mice Mansion Takeaway ?

I expect you soon to call,
For nice mice meals are waiting for you all,
To dine in the Banqueting Hall !

So, come on down !
Leave house, field and barn !
Its time to hunt and play
at Mice Mansion Takeaway !

The Cat Who Would Not Sit on the Mat

He growled and glared if you dare sat
In the fireside chair of Claud the cat,
And if you remained
He further complained
By tearing the weave out of the mat !

Barn Ratter

Buster had the poorest chance,
The gasping runt of the litter.
Later, when spurned by his mother,
He was kept to be the barn ratter.

High in the great barn loft,
Buster made his humble croft.
There he sleeps, washes and eats.
Mice and rats supply his daily feast.

He never lingers near the house,
Stays close to geese and grouse.
When the children ask him to play,
Buster growls and runs away.

In waving fields he'll silently hide,
Listening for the tiniest sound.
He hears the horses on their ride
And, right behind, Lennie the hound.

Buster, once, briefly disappeared,
In an attempt to extend his crown.
But limped back with a bleeding nose
Inflicted by opponents unknown.

His yellow eyes burn in the dark.
A sudden leap and a sudden squeal
Reveals the resident barn ratter,
Has caught another moonlit meal.

As winter turns cold and raw
He burrows deeper into the straw,
Where he dreams and gently snores
While gales shake the great barn doors.

Kitten in a Sock

Terri had five kids
And loved every single one,
But still grounded Darren
For something really nasty he'd done.

Darren felt such hatred for his mum,
Revenge raged in his mind.
What sweeter than one of the kittens ?
The cutest he could find.

Into his step dad's sock
He rammed the mewing kitten -
Slapped it hard against his bedroom wall
Then tossed it into the bin.

Terri declared she was horrified
Her son displayed a murderous rage.
Though nothing could be done
As the perpetrator was under age.

Feline Defence

What could be more absurder
Than to accuse me of murder ?
How could they be so vile,
For I far prefer to purr and smile ?

Actually, I'm so very, very.........nice.
Though, I admit, I've a problem with mice.
But they always make ladies scared,
So why should their lives be spared ?

I've also heard rather disparaging words
Concerning my attitude towards birds.
In fact, what am I supposed to do ?
If birds get upset - well, let them sue !

And, another thing - bug-eyed goldfish !
As if they're a sitting target - I wish !
My poor paw can hardly get in the hole
They leave in the gold fish bowl !

And its almost a myth, a legend, a fable,
That I'd steal meat off the kitchen table !
So, I must admit I'm confused and hurt,
That I should be taken to court !

But I'm ready to be put to the test,
For I know My Defence will be best !
Just remember, I shall not be alone -
I'll call the owners of my home.

And also my friends and supporters,
Who will absolve me of all slaughters.
And, though, I have minor, predatory flaws,
Who doesn't who has teeth and claws ?

I always play fair in every possible way,
Look how I let that spider run away !
And my loving attitude to my owners,
Shows I'm not one of those
serial cat killer loners !

Although, now I'm coming up to five,
I still love to share what I catch alive !
I must admit I'm so very well known
For bringing my trophies back home !

What about that rat I placed on the floor,
Who ran up to Gran against the door ?
Or the scream of delight from Mum,
When she saw in my mouth that robin ?

Or the lizard I held that made Mum yell
For Dad to come and see as well !
Or the little girl's magnificent squeal,
When I dragged in a bunny for my meal ?

In fact, I'm so very good and kind,
No more generous creature could you find !
So, please don't bark at me anymore,
For I'm only upholding Natural Cat Law !

Rich Pussy

If you believe in rags to riches,
This cat tale will have you in stitches !

One afternoon a stray cat
Walked through an open window,
And into the house and heart of Mrs Walker,
an elderly widow.

She named the stray, Pussy,
And treated her like a queen -
Providing the best chairs and the best food
any cat has ever seen !

Pussy wasn't complaining, life had become
so entertaining !

The stray cat had won the equivalent of the lottery:
Scottish salmon for breakfast
Or roe on toast,
While caviare for dinner helped her get thinner.
And, to help her sleep, on a snow white satin sheet.

When Mrs Walker died,
She generously supplied
An animal charity with three million pounds
Through properties and securities alone,
On the condition they found Pussy
A VERY GOOD HOME !

Mrs Walker need not have had any fears,
For her wealth was enough to keep in good health
an average cat
2,236 years !

Animal Shelter - Cat Wing

The new wing's been superbly done.
Nothing here annoys.
They've got space to climb and run,
And a range of toys
To chase and tug when they want fun.

They have their own compartment
With a white front door.
A cushioned basket with a blanket
And food galore,
Besides assured access to a vet.

They've also heat when it turns cold
And a fan when its hot.
Its adaptable to suit young and old.
No more wood will rot.
The standards attained deserve gold.

They've got their names written out
On cards next to the door -
Randall, Samson, Jonty stand about.
Some leap onto the floor,
While others sleep or mew or pout.

There's nothing more to really achieve.
But when left alone,
Old cats, sick cats, difficult cats grieve,
Because from this home
Some sense they will never ever leave.

Moustache, the Soldiers' Cat

This is not cat folk lore
As it occurred during the First World War -
When Moustache, the cat, stayed in a trench
Amid fatal danger, mud and stench !

Belgium soldiers confirmed,
Even the rats were heard to squirm !
Moustache was a potential victim for shells
That were greeted with screams and yells !

Despite being bombarded night and day,
Moustache never ran away !
He stayed at his post when bullets flew
Though he only responded with a mew !

Besides war-weary soldiers he sat near
And never shed a single tear !
A dapper little puss so very brave,
Despite mortar pounding wave after wave !

He caught rats running around
And hiding in shelters' underground.
He stayed with the regiment throughout the war
And when peace occurred, no doubt, purred !

Moustache was then placed in a loving home,
While nationally known
As the Soldiers' Friend,
And became a beloved Belgium legend !

Churchill's War Cats

Is there anything more to possibly tell
About the War and Winston Churchill ?
Of course there is, and its the little known story
Of those who were called Nelson and Smokey !

You might ask who on earth were they ?
No less than Churchill's feline friends night and day !
For throughout the Second World War,
Cats strolled 10 Downing Street's famous floors.

Though the question has never been raised before,
What did those cats contribute to winning the war ?
Nelson and Smokey were sufficently important,
To attend meetings of the War Cabinet !

When in the First Lord of the Admiralty's flat,
Churchill adopted Nelson, the Admiralty's cat.
A big, black, regal feline who slept on the bed,
Where he was thoughtfully patted on the head.

Nelson regularly witnessed bedside dications
And astounded visiting Admirals' expectations !
When Churchill moved as PM into Number Ten,
He was accompanied by the navy's cat, Nelson.

Nelson's war contribution affirmed by Churchill,
Who declared he was helping to save valuable fuel.
And the War Cat Effort a new Nelson led,
By acting as a hot water bottle on the PM's bed !

Though Nelson was afraid of anti-aircraft guns
And hid under the bed during air raids on London.
But Churchill told Nelson to be valiant in war
And to emulate the heroic name the cat bore !

No matter how dark the day, humour never failed,
When near a window, Nelson would wave his tail.
The PM suggested it was a message in semaphore
To enemy agents waiting with a U-boat off shore !

Smokey witnessed decisions on crucial events
And, maybe, he mewed to indicate his agreement.
Across Top Secret Dossiers did he quietly creep
And over Invasion Europe plans suddenly leap ?

Whatever else is said about Smokey and Nelson,
They helped the heart that fought for freedom;
And offered precious comfort the War deferred,
When on Mr Churchill's bed they laid down and purred.

The Cat Art of Chilling Out

Have you time to consider how cats chill ?
It may prevent you getting ill !

Have you noticed Custard ignoring every call,
Because he's asleep on the garden wall ?

Have you listened to how Sasha starts to purr
Whenever we cuddle her ?

Have you noticed Ronnie stretching everything
Like a furry, uncoiled spring ?

Have you heard Hamlet snore,
When wedged under the bedroom radiator ?

Have you watched Jelly curled up on the bed
With a paw over her head ?

Have you observed Socks flat out on the settee,
But always wakes up just in time for tea ?

Have you seen Charles basking in the glow
When sunlight pours through the window ?

And have you been told owning a cat
Helps your nerves and your heart ?

Cat Debt Repaid

Roger was a senior citizen
Who woke one freezing winter night.
The electric heater had broken down !
His glass of water - a solid, icy weight !

Suffering from hypothermia -
He couldn't reach his bedside light !
At four in the morning it could be said,
Roger looked as if he'd soon be dead !

Until Misty, his overweight Turkish Angora Blue,
Jumped up and settled on Roger's chest !
And the warmth from his heavy, furry weight
Meant Roger survived winter's deadliest test !

She lay like a hot water bottle across
His shivering, wheezing chest,
And licked and nuzzled Roger‘s face,
So he'd not fall into that fatal, frozen rest !

Roger soon felt strong enough to reach out
And switch on the electric blanket.
But, then, dropped the cable on the floor -
Only for Misty to lift it back up with her paw !

At last, he switched on the blanket,
And no longer felt under threat.
Roger rang the bell to alert his wife,
And declared Misty had saved his life !

Yet, they'd nursed Misty back to health
When she was a kitten gasping for breath.
Seven years later, Misty repaid them
By rescuing Roger from a freezing death !

Fast Eddie, Street Cat

Fast Eddie's got no time for you or me.
He's a street cat, fighting fit and free,
And snarls at two-legged company.

Black and grey stripes suit his style
For he gets dirty
Tramping mile after mile.

Over walls he leaps and dives.
Long ago he used up his nine lives.
Yet, still survives.

His home he hates,
Since the eldest boy kicked him in the face.
A battered garden shed his new place.

He's been shot by an air gun
And many a stone just missed his crown.
But he's overcome everything and everyone.

He'll never settle down - are you mad ?
For with girls Fast Eddie is a bit of a lad.
Some would say even a cad !

Eddie doesn't mind A Loving Home missed.
He'd hate to be stroked and kissed.
He's wedded to Dare and Risk.

Eddie's got his tricks-
If thirsty, dew from grass licks.
Snatches spiders for a fast food fix.

Fast Eddie travels far.
He excels at dodging cars
Or using them to sleep under the stars.

He's got no time for a night's rest
For rival cats are always ready to test
Whether Fast Eddie is still the best.

His idea of delight
Is a bite from the bins
Followed by a late night fight.

Most scraps end in a tie.
One opponent lost an eye,
Who Eddie hoped would also die.

Fast Eddie's life may not be very nice
But he reckons its full of spice.
No cat has challenged him twice.

And for this great little lion,
Nothing quite beats
His Hard Old Life on the Streets !

Battling Zak

Our weary veteran of battles and wars,
Which we can reckon up in scores !
And we know Zak
Will always attack,
Until he loses all his teeth and claws !

Wilma, the Quiet Cat

I'm not the sort who stands out.
    I keep myself to myself.
Though you might see me about,
    Smiling on the window shelf.

I'm not the sort who likes to parade.
    I like life sedate and calm,
And much prefer the gentle shade,
    Far from any fuss or alarm.

I'm not the sort whose a star
    And would never wander far.
I like staying at home
    And through rooms quietly roam.

I'm not the sort to hiss -
    That Drama Queen stuff I'll miss.
Even when I purr,
    Not even a butterfly would stir.

I'm not the sort to make a scene,
    I only like to keep warm and clean.
I hide behind the settee when I hear
    Strange voices coming near.

I'm not the sort to show off.
    I like my comfy chair near the fire,
Where I can lay in the buff
    And among sweet dreams retire.

Cotsall Tossel

A depressed, disgruntled She
Whose life had gone as wrong as it could be -
Her lady owner had died
And, so, her nephew took her for a ride
To a place unknown -
The town's Animal Rescue Home.

She stayed longer than any cat,
And everyday quietly and miserably sat.
Among the outcast
It seemed her life was doomed to last,
For no one wanted her -
An old cat who refused to purr.

Until an old bachelor came
Who staked Tossel for his claim.
In November cold
He drove her back high into the Cotswold,
To his twin cottage home
Where Tossel learned to reign and roam.

A solitary kind of chap,
Who stroked her when she sat on his lap.
In return Tossel never
Gave trouble all the time they lived together,
Which stayed the same,
Until her cancer five years later came.

Elegy for Tossel

The diagnosis came as a shock -
Malignant growth in the back of her throat,
Which caused her purring to be so deep.

When weight loss started to occur
Her body became a sponge of fur.
Yet, still she mewed and still she purred.

She looked for a way out of the surgery.
But there was no escape from her disease.
This time I could not rescue her.

In her last two years deafness had loomed.
Signalled by a startled cry if, to soon,
I suddenly came into the room.

The oldest cat at the Rescue Home,
Until I adopted her five years ago.
She became my unrivalled, feline Queen.

Even when I cuddled her to say goodbye
Tossel roused herself to be bright-eyed.
She even purred before she died.

I should be grateful for those five years
For Tossel was such a soothing companion,
Affirmed in the tribute of tears.

Yet, the gulf at home feels the worst,
Which only amplifies her loss -
When unconditional love is given and lost.

Loss of a Pet

How can one explain
The sense of loss, the sense of pain,
Just how upset
An owner can be at the loss of a pet ?

They quickly say,
"You'll get over it ! You'll soon be okay !"
But what can be said,
When the pet you've loved is dead ?

More than a pet, surely.
More than a friend, part of the family !
A small life, long or brief,
Their worth demonstrated by such grief.

Others declare
Human company needs most care;
But pets climb above,
For they give unquestioning love.

They teach us things
About what true relationships brings:
Unrivalled sincerity,
Bond builders of trust and loyalty.

We'll never be apart,
What was offered holds in our heart.
And in fond memory will stay,
Until we, too, are summoned away.

Baby Rescue

Despite a cold, and howling night wind,
Fluffy the Persian refused to come in !
She persistently miaowed and cried
Until her owner, a Nurse, followed her outside !

But the east wind blew so bitterly cold
Onto her cape the Nurse had to hold,
And to her cat spoke rather gruffly,
"This really had better be worth it, Fluffy !"

She led her owner to a bundle under a bush,
Which the Nurse thought just a load of rubbish !
But Fluffy loudly miaowed, until the nurse saw
A tiny, pink hand next to Fluffy's paw !

As she uncovered the bundle she heard,
What she first thought was incredibly absurd,
But, as a nurse, knew so well that sound -
It was a whimpering baby her cat had found !

Unlike the real mother, Fluffy had stayed,
Until the abandoned baby had been rescued.
The Nurse gathered the baby in her arms
And took it to hospital to be safe from harm.

The real mother was never found but that
Did not foil Fluffy, the Heroic Persian cat,
Whose maternal instincts caused her mews
To be praised in the press
and television news !

Felix the Phoenix

Due to an alleged rent dispute,
It was like giant against a mouse
As the JCB driver vented his rage
By bulldozing the Landlord's house !

Inside, a terrified dog and five cats
Could stand it no more -
And leapt through a crumbling bay window
Before gave way the upstairs floor !

The digger crushed and smashed
Every single room, hall and kitchen !
Until the house finally collapsed
And spilled onto the lawns and garden !

But Ashley, the seven year old,
Grey Korat cat did not leap outside.
So, when the house collapsed,
They believed Ashley was still inside !

After the dust had settled it was clear
The extent of the damage was great.
Their lovely house was demolished
And with it their sweet Korat's fate !

The owners were more distressed
Over Ashley, their prized and beloved pet,
Than the mountain of rubble from their home,
Which, they knew, could be rebuilt.

The owners wept knowing Ashley
Had faced a terrifying death alone;
And, worse, that such a dreadful end,
Happened in the family's lovely home.

Their six surviving pets were all in shock.
The dog wailed and five cats mewed,
Not only for the loss of their home
But also Ashley, whom they all loved.

Yet, the following day at lunchtime,
A policeman spied Ashley's grey outline,
Huddled near a half-hanging door
On the edge of a tottering floor !

Ashley looked like a tiny grey ghost
Perched on the brink of sudden death !
The fire brigade went straight into action,
While onlookers held their breath !

They soon rescued a very dusty Ashley,
And his owners' hearts were filled with joy,
When they held him close in their arms
For Ashley was their favourite feline boy !

Terrifed, he'd stayed under a bed,
Which just managed to keep him alive !
Though, once the welcome was over,
He mewed for food to help him revive !

So, even when a house is bulldozed,
And its prize cat is inside when it crashes,
Ashley demonstrated it can still survive -
Like Felix the Phoenix rising above the ashes !

Dangerous Laughter

Never, never, never ever laugh at a cat,
Nothing causes more humiliation than that !
A betrayal felt so great,
That you'll suddenly rate
Not just below dog but also a sewer rat !

Feline Killer

Sea blue, July sky, crystal clear.
Sunniest day of the year.
Holy Day, too. People amble past.
Peace has come to the world at last.

And, then, up onto the window sill
Scamp, the cat, presents her kill !
Her pale green eyes offer not a hint of grief
As she clutches the sparrow in her teeth !

Bird, rat or mouse -
Scamp would love to bring it into the house !
But the dangling head of the little bird,
Indicates, though warm, she's dead.

This morning her last song she sung.
So, the front window is shut with a bang !
Scamp jumps down with hurt surprise,
And into the hedge carries her prize.

Yet, ten minutes ago you'd have heard
How she sat on my lap and quietly purred.
Though, who could believe at that time,
She was about to commit the greatest crime.

What hurts so much is that the feline
Who's the Murderess is MINE !
But like all cat owners prone to speeches,
Its my cat who truly teaches:

The Royal Hunt by the Cat remains,
Favoured by all Felines;
For what they do is as old as the sun,
And will always be done by cat or lion.

Too Fat, Too Thin

Fat Cat got sent to the vet,
And ordered to go on a crash diet -
For if Fat Cat was fed anymore,
He'd be anchored to the floor !

Fat Cat started to get thin,
And after six months was so slim
He could climb what he pleased
And loved scaring birds off trees !

His owners said that was wrong
Because they liked bird song !
Too fat, too thin ? How can cat win ?
By deciding - as always -
Just to do his own thing !

Slim - formerly Fat - Cat
Decided tinned food
Was not really all that good !
So he went out in all weathers,
Hunting warm meat under feathers.

But his owners never knew
Fresh bird was the most popular dish
On Thin Cat's
Health conscious new menu !

So, when it came to din, din, din,
For Thin Cat it was win, win, win !

Hard to Please Siamese

How can we ever please
Cindy our Siamese ?
Who makes it blatantly known
She's the Real Boss of Our Home ?

Who mews, then sighs,
While her sky-blue eyes hypnotise ?
Who weaves a spell so very well,
Yet can yell as though from Hell ?

Who loves to be stroked on the head,
But who'll suddenly scram instead ?
Who has meals served on time
And tastier than her owners' sometimes ?

Who must be politely greeted,
And insists on being fussed and feted ?
Who has a heart-churning howl
And a temper most foul ?

Who's so haughty
And can be truly naughty ?
Who loves talking on the phone
And loathes being left alone ?

Who insists on being carried on shoulders
And likes to sleep on files and folders ?
Who rejects best bits of meat
And most of our friends refuses to greet ?

Yet, who runs across the floor
To greet us when we open the door ?
And, once we're inside our place,
Wants to be kissed and embraced ?

The Jazz Cats

Trad jazz stomps and shakes in the bar
For weekly customers from near and far.
Trombones and clarinets rise and fall,
Pass right through the stone built wall.

But Marmite the pub cat plays it cool
And carries on washing on the bar stool !

Every single seat within moments taken
For lunch time live music in the making.
The winking drummer strikes up the beat,
Everyone's swinging and tapping their feet.

Marmite the cat doesn't complain,
To him each tune sounds much the same !

The standard classics are given their due,
Even some tunes written brand new.
But nothing beats the sound of a horn,
Which sparkles in ears no matter how worn !

Though Marmite the cat yawns and stretches,
And below his left ear briefly scratches.

Foot-tapping folk come from far and near,
For live music, the company and real beer.
The trad band hits notes high and clean,
As fine as found in the heart of New Orleans !

But Marmite the cat stops in his tracks
When Elmo, his brother, taps his back !

Though places are few and far between,
To Marmite and Elmo folk are never mean.
They squeeze along to create space to fit,
So Elmo next to Marmite can easily sit !

Marmite the cat finally demurs,
Curls up in a corner and raps out his purrs.

The air crackles with such red-hot tunes,
It makes January feel like flaming June !
And customers express appreciation
With applause for a two minute duration !

We're sure you'll love our Sunday jazz show,
With those real jazz cats, Marmite and Elmo !

So, if you think you, too, are a cool cat,
Then grab your coat and put on your hat !
We'll see you down here next Sunday,
Where hot cats listen to jazz being played !

So blow that horn, strum that bass, hit that note,
And we'll see if you're a cat who'll sink or float !

The Naunton Three

What a winning threesome in Naunton to find,
Who stroll every morning with a similar mind:
Toby, the spaniel,
His owner as well,
And Nora, their russet cat, following behind !

The Wild Cat of Scotland

I've read so many tales about this cat,
    Utterly resistant to human contact !
He hates with a fire strong as the sun,
    Anything man has ever done !

Uncrowned King among feral types,
    With a tabby coat and dark stripes.
Sometimes seen hunting in sunlight,
    But prefers to range late at night.

He silently stalks through a wood
    And wears its shade like a hood,
The only thing that halts any surprise
    Is the ghostly light in his moon eyes !

The Scottish Lion of Kingdom Glen,
    Happiest when far away from men.
Master hunter after doe, hare, bird,
    Causes their last cries to be heard !

He'll growl, hiss, counter and attack
    Those who dare block his track.
He'll convert a domestic cat at will
    From purring tabby into feral devil !

His destiny we shall never know -
    At home among storm and snow.
The cat only highland eagles detect.
    Yet, what other wins such respect ?

And its future survival we also wish,
With the motto of Clan Mackintosh
For the Scottish beastie they love -
'Touch not the cat except with a glove'.

The Stray

She was there yesterday.
Perhaps she wants to stay.

And seems to know,
I'm watching her from the window.

She's looks tired and thin.
With cats I never win.

They choose you -
Unerringly true !

And, from what I see,
She's targeted me.

Typical mug, once again.
I finally obey and let her in.

Now she won't go away,
No matter what I say.

But, no longer at home,
Do I feel alone.

West Beach Cats, Adelaide

Where rocks tower over the beach,
Abandoned cats have made their home.
These furtive felines remain out of reach,
Where high tides rarely rise and roam.

Among gaps, fissures and cracks,
Safe from dog and storm attacks,
The beach cats survive daily duress
Within stone harbours of darkness.

Self survival skills instantly teach
Once dumped by transient tenants.
Cats control their rim of West Beach,
Establish territorial tribal haunts.

No longer mingle, meek and mild,
Here they've turned wary and wild.
Yet, on the rocks idle and sunbathe,
Above the fall of a neighbouring wave.

A shady bush spitefully cut to a reed
Is where a few perform a kinder deed -
True supporters of an abandoned breed,
Apportion tinned food for them to feed.

After three weeks of an outstretched hand,
A black and grey tabby tom understands:
One old lady still wants to be their friend
And their banishment put to an end.

Letting Freddie Out

All day he has slept.
And, now, when we turn off the telly,
Draw tight the curtains,
Switch off the light,
He goes and stands by the kitchen door,
Awaiting his release.

When we're ready for bed
He demonstrates his built-in pedigree.
Eager to get out, scout about,
Stalk spooky shadows.
He barely looks at us.
Psyching himself up for the Dark.

We open the kitchen door
To be greeted by cold, hostile air.
He pauses and sniffs.
Reading a host of things out there.
We will never see or smell,
Touch or hear.

Within seconds he's changed
His shape, identity, character.
No more our puss, our Freddie.
He lowers his black and white body
And slinks quietly out,
Like a furry submarine into black waters.

A silent, soundless assassin.
Senses as alert as radar.
Smaller things fear his sensors.
Amber eyes reveal his presence.
His teeth rival razors.
His claws keen to rip, tear, maul.

They Revert at Night

More than Darkness.
Show Time !

More than a house.
The Den.

More than lawns and gardens.
Veldt and Jungle.

More than rodents.
Deer and Gazelles.

More than roads and paths.
Tracks and Borders.

More than walls.
Mountain ranges.

More than the neighbourhood.
The Battleground.

More than shadows.
Prey or Enemy.

More than cats.
Lion and Lioness.

Nine Lives

i

To be sired by a suitor
Before its neutered.

ii

To find a home and be accepted
Or be lethally injected.

iii

To escape a mistress or master,
Who'll make life a disaster.

iv

To by-pass serious wheezes
And fatal cat diseases.

v

To dodge lorries and cars
That cause amputees and scars.

vi

To avoid troublesome toms at night
And survive feuds and fights.

vii

To evade cruelty as well
By Lesser Humanoids from Hell.

viii

To get into a jam, fix or scrape,
Yet still escape !

ix

The Ninth Supreme Escape,
Save for the Grave:

And who can possibly doubt,
The Spirit of Cat

WILL LEAP OUT !

References

ANDERSON, Janice. *Cat Calls* (Enfield, Middlesex: Guinness Publishing)

CHURCHILL Museum and War Cabinet Rooms, London

COOPER, Jilly. *Animals in War* (London: William Heinemann)

CUTTS, Paddy. *The Practical Cat Book* (London: Hermes House)

DAWS, Karen. *Cat Calls* (London: Weidenfeld and Nicolson)

DITZ. *A Collection of Cats Tales* (London: AAPPL)

GREENE, David. *Incredible Cats* (London: Methuen)

HALLS, Vicky. *Cat Confidential* (London: Bantam Books)

HARRIS, Rolf. *True Animal Tales* (London: Century)

KORDA, Michael. and KORDA, Margaret. *Cat People* (London: Hodder and Stoughton)

LEHMAN, Jill and Martin. *Cat Portraits* (London: Pelham Books)

LEWIS, Martin. *Cats in the News* (London: Warner Books)

MACBETH, George. & BOOTH, Martin. *The Book of Cats* (London: Secker and Warburg)
MORRIS, Desmond. *Catlore* (London: Jonathan Cape)

MORRIS, Desmond. *Catwatching* (London: Jonathan Cape)

O'CONNELL, Hugh. *Cotswold Cats* (Bourton on the Water,Gloucestershire: Cygnet Press)

REID, Beryl. *The Cat's Whiskers* (London: Ebury Press)

ROWSE, A. L. *A Quartet of Cornish Cats* (London: Weidenfeld and Nicolson)

SCHNECK, Marcus. & CARAVAN, Jill. *Cat Facts* (London: Quantum Publishing)

TABOR, Roger. *Understanding Cats* (Newton Abbot, Devon: David and Charles)

TANGYE, Derek. *Somewhere A Cat Is Waiting* (London: Sphere Books)

TAYLOR, David. & MARTYN, Elizabeth. *The Little Tabby Cat Book* (London: Dorling Kindersley)

www.ingramcontent.com/pod-product-compliance
Ingram Content Group UK Ltd.
Pitfield, Milton Keynes, MK11 3LW, UK
UKHW041847190726
13854UKWH00002B/756